LETTER

TO

HON. WILLIAM NELSON, M. C.,

ON

MR. WEBSTER'S SPEECH,

FROM

WILLIAM JAY.

New-York:

WILLIAM HARNED, 61 JOHN STREET.

Price 2 cts. single; 18¾ cts. a dozen; $1 00 a hundred.

1850.

LETTER.

NEW YORK, 16th March, 1850.

MY DEAR SIR:—Availing myself of your kind invitation to give you my sentiments at any time, on topics occupying the attention of Congress, I wrote to you a few weeks ago, in relation to the compromise proposed by Mr. Clay. Since the date of that letter, you, and I, and indeed the whole nation, have been astounded by the strange course pursued in the Senate by Mr. Webster. I inquire not into his motives; to his own master he standeth or falleth: but certainly it must be admitted by friends and foes, that his recent somerset is one of the boldest and most extraordinary ever thrown by a political tumbler. I will not inflict upon you a minute examination of his lamentable speech, but I will take the liberty to call your attention to a few of its prominent points.

Gen. Cass frankly confessed that, with regard to the Wilmot proviso, "a change had come over him"; but Mr. Webster, while his personal identity is almost wholly destroyed, while scarcely a fragment of the former man remains, is under the hallucination that he is the same Daniel Webster as before, and while denouncing and ridiculing the proviso, professes to be as much devoted to its principle as ever!

He *now* pours contempt, not only upon legislative instructions, but also upon legislative expressions of hostility to the extension of slavery. "I should be unwilling to receive from the Legislature of Massachusetts any instructions to *present* resolutions *expressive of any opinions whatever, on the subject of slavery,* for two reasons: first, I do not consider that the Legislature of Massachusetts has anything to do with it; and next, I do not consider that I, as her representative, have anything to do with it."

On the 1st of March, 1847, he read in the Senate certain strong anti-slavery resolutions of the Massachusetts Legislature, and announced that they had been passed *unanimously.* Did he then rebuke the Legislature of his State, for meddling with what was none of their business? Hear him: "I THANK her (Massachusetts) for it, and am PROUD of her, for she has denounced the whole object for which our armies are now traversing the mountains of Mexico. If anything is certain, it is that the sentiment of the whole North is utterly opposed to the acquisition of territory to be formed into *new slaveholding States.*"—*Cong. Globe, p. 555.*

In 1819, Mr. Webster, as one of the committee, submitted to a Boston meeting two resolutions, viz.: "That the Congress of the United States possess the constitutional power, upon the admission of any new State created beyond the limits of the original territory of the United States, to make the prohibition of the further extension of slavery or involuntary servitude in such new State a condition of its admission;" and that "It is just and expedient that this power *should be exercised by Congress* upon the admission of ALL new States erected beyond the original limits of the United States." *Now* Mr. Webster, as the representative of Massachusetts in Congress, does not consider that *he* has anything to do with the subject of slavery!

When it was ascertained, during the war, that new territory would be acquired, and when it was openly avowed that it was to become slave territory, the House of Representatives passed Mr. Wilmot's proviso, expressly excluding slavery from the territory to be thus acquired. This, as we all know, led to a violent political agitation. What part did Mr. Webster take in this agitation? In 1847, he addressed a meeting of his own party, and declared, "There is not a man in this hall WHO HOLDS TO THE PRINCIPLE OF THE WILMOT PROVISO MORE FIRMLY THAN I DO." The principle of the proviso was the exclusion of slavery, by act of Congress, from *the territory to be acquired from Mexico;* and that territory, we all know, was none other than New-Mexico and California.

The agitation waxed fiercer and fiercer. The Whig party at the North pledged themselves to the proviso; the Legislature of Massachusetts, as we have seen, *unanimously* declared for the exclusion of slavery from New-Mexico and California, and Mr. Webster publicly thanked his State, and was proud of her for so doing. The Whig party in Massachusetts nominated Mr. Webster for the Presidency, and he stood before the country as the *Wilmot proviso candidate.* General Taylor was ultimately selected as the Whig candidate, and was supported by the Northern Whigs, on the pledges made by his friends, that he would not veto the proviso. General Cass, on the other hand, was the avowed anti-proviso candidate, and as such, was opposed by the whole Whig party at the North. The great issue on which the election turned in the free States, was the prohibition or permission, by Congress, of slavery in New-Mexico and California. After the candidates were nominated, and while the whole country was convulsed with this issue, what was the course of Mr. Webster? Did he dissent from his Northern friends? Did he tell them the issue they had made was a nonsensical one? Hear him once more. On the 10th of August, 1848, *after* New-Mexico and California were acquired, he rose in the Senate and thus delivered himself: "My opposition to the increase of slavery in this country, or to the increase of slave representation, is general and universal. It has no reference to the lines of *latitude* or points of the compass. I SHALL OPPOSE ALL SUCH EXTENSION AT ALL TIMES AND UNDER ALL CIRCUMSTANCES, EVEN AGAINST ALL INDUCEMENTS, AGAINST ALL SUPPOSED LIMITATION OF GREAT INTERESTS, AGAINST ALL COMBINATIONS, AGAINST ALL COMPROMISES."

To what, let me ask, did this solemn, emphatic, unqualified asseveration refer? Did he then know that there was not a foot of territory in the United States, over which it was not morally and physically impossible to extend slavery? Was he promising, in these impressive terms, to oppose what he was conscious would never be attempted? Did he make this pledge before his country, with a mental reservation to unite hereafter with General Cass and the slaveholders, in denouncing and scorning the proviso? Did he mean to deceive his own party? Did he desire to keep up an angry agitation, throughout the nation, for electioneering purposes, and did he thus intimate his belief in the danger of the extension of slavery and slave representation, when he well knew that the fiat of the Almighty had rendered such extension impossible? Was he then acquainted with the "law of physical geography," which would render the proviso "a re-enactment of the will of God?" And did he purposely conceal the secret of this law in his own breast, when, by revealing it, he might have stilled the raging billows of popular passion which threatened to engulf the Union? To suppose all this, would be to impute to Mr. Webster a degree of trickery and turpitude rarely paralleled even among politicians. Hence we are bound to assume that the law of nature, on which he *now* relies, is a recent discovery, subsequent at least to the 10th August, 1848

It is, however, extraordinary, that a gentleman of his acquirements did not sooner become acquainted with this "LAW OF PHYSICAL GEOGRAPHY—THE LAW OF THE FORMATION OF THE EARTH, THAT SETTLES FOR EVER, BEYOND ALL TERMS OF HUMAN ENACTMENT, THAT SLAVERY CANNOT EXIST IN CALIFORNIA OR NEW-MEXICO." It is to be regretted that Mr. Webster did not condescend to demonstrate the existence of this law, and to explain the mode of its operation. He, indeed, tells us that our new territories are "Asiatic in their formation and scenery;" but this fact does not prove his law, since slavery has existed for ages amid the scenery of Asia; it exists in the deserts of Africa, has existed in every country of Europe, and now exists in the frozen regions of Russia. This law, moreover, must have been enacted by the Creator since 1824, or its operation must have been previously suspended in deference to the Spanish government; for under that government, negro slavery did exist in New-Mexico and California, and it ceased in 1824, not by the law of "physical geography," but by a Mexican edict. Thousands of slaves are employed in the mines of Brazil, and Mr. Webster does not explain how his law forbids their employment in the mines of California. Mr. Webster ridicules the application of the proviso to Canada, in case of annexation. I neither see nor feel the point of his wit—slavery is already prohibited by the local law of Canada, but were it not, most certainly it ought to be prohibited as a condition of annexation. New-York adjoins Canada, and Mr. Webster probably regards the prohibition of slavery in our recent Constitution as the height of absurdity. In 1790 there were 21,000 slaves in New-York, and on the 4th of July, 1827, about 10,000 slaves were emancipated, not by Mr. Webster's law, but by act of the Legislature, and the number would have been much greater, had not laws for their gradual emancipation been in operation since 1796. For a long period, slavery flourished in New-York undisturbed by abolitionists. The absence of all anti-slavery agitation was as perfect as Mr. Webster's heart could desire. Stray negroes were caught with almost as much ease as stray pigs. Neither pulpit nor press ruffled the happy serenity of the slaveholders. But this blissful repose was suddenly broken in 1741, by rumors of an *intended* insurrection. Courts and executioners were immediately put into requisition, and in pursuance of judicial sentences, *thirteen slaves were burnt alive at the stake in the city of New-York*, eighteen were hanged, and seventy-one were exported to foreign markets. Mr. Webster is unnecessarily distressed by the supposed unhappy influence of the anti-slavery agitation upon the condition of the slaves. They were never better treated, were never less miserable than at the present moment. The more public observation is directed to the conduct of the masters, the less reprehensible will that conduct be.

The promulgation of the law of "physical geography" seems to make no impression on the slaveholders, as they continue as ravenous as ever for the new territories. But with one accord they unite with the pro-slavery Democrats at the North, and with our Northern politicians and merchants eager for Southern votes and Southern trade, in lauding and glorifying him, not for his discovery of a new law of nature, but for his discovery of a NATIONAL PLEDGE to receive into the Union THREE SLAVE STATES to be formed out of the Texan territory—for his denunciation of the proviso, and for his promised aid in catching the future Latimers who may be found on the soil of MASSACHUSETTS.

Congress by the Constitution may admit new States at discretion, and hence new States have been admitted on various conditions. The joint resolutions admitting Texas imposed *restrictions* on this power. Congress *may*, with the consent of Texas, admit *one* State north of 36° 30′, but if admitted, it *must* be as a free State. Congress *may* admit *three* States, with the consent of Texas, south of that line; but if admitted, no restriction in regard to slavery can be imposed on them. Mr. Webster now finds in these resolutions what had escaped the knowledge of both the North and the South, viz., a NATIONAL PLEDGE to admit THREE SLAVE STATES. As no State can be admitted without the consent of Texas, and as that consent will be withheld for a State north of 36° 30′, it follows, according to Mr. Webster, that we have made a one-sided bargain; of the four contemplated States, we *must* have three with slavery, but are to be cheated out of the one with freedom. This discovery, which has taken the whole nation by surprise, is, like the discovery of the geographical law, of recent date.

On the 22d March, 1848, Mr. Webster was ignorant of this national pledge! In his speech in the Senate, on that day, alluding to the joint resolutions, he remarked:—

"If you refer to the resolutions providing for the annexation of Texas, you find a proviso that it shall be in the POWER OF CONGRESS hereafter to make four new States out of the Texan territory—present and prospective five new States; ten new Senators MAY come into the Union out of Texas."—*Houston's Reports*, p. 403.

Mr. Webster pledges himself to vote for the bill now pending in the Senate, for the recovery of fugitive slaves, by which a citizen of Massachusetts may be converted into a beast of burden, and by which any man or woman may be made to pay $1,500, and be confined six months in prison, for the crime of giving food and lodging, harboring and concealing a fellow-being, and perhaps a fellow-Christian, guiltless of crime, and thus aiding him in the pursuit of life, liberty and happiness. Possibly Mr. Webster may hereafter discover a law of human nature that will render this pledge as worthless as his geographical law has rendered his proviso pledge. Let us inquire into the practical working of this proposed law. As Mr. Webster is to vote for it, he, of course, can have no conscientious objection to aid in executing it. Let us then imagine a scene in perfect consistency with the position he has assumed.

On his return from Washington, he is followed by Messrs. Bruin and Hill, who retain him in a prosecution they have commenced against a Boston matron. She had harbored their beautiful slave, for whom they had lately demanded eighteen hundred dollars, and who had effected her escape from bondage and outrage. The cause is ready for trial, not before a postmaster or other solitary official, but, as in this case it *must be*, before a BOSTON JURY. The Court is opened, and the jury empanelled; but the room is thronged to suffocation, and an anxious multitude without is striving for admittance. A cry is heard—To FANEUIL HALL! The Court yields to the wishes of the people. The lady, guarded by constables, and DANIEL WEBSTER, locked arm in arm with his Alexandria clients, wend their way to the Hall. The judges and jury have taken their seats, the old Cradle of Liberty is filled to its utmost capacity with citizens of Boston, the silence of the grave pervades the vast assembly, but men's hearts are beating with unwonted violence, and scorn and indignation are distorting the lineaments of every countenance. DANIEL WEBSTER rises as counsel for the prosecution, and Hancock and Warren, and the Adamses, and other apostles and martyrs of New-England liberty, seem to look down upon him from their canvas with unnatural sternness. The feed advocate of the slave traders turns to the jury with some little embarrassment of manner, some tremor of muscle. He commences his address with a learned exposition of the Constitution. Next follows a soul-stirring eulogium upon our GLORIOUS UNION—the last hope of freedom, the refuge for the oppressed of all the nations upon earth. Most earnestly does he protest that no man abominates slavery more than he does; and to prove his sincerity, he quotes from his *old* speeches, and repeats his *old* pledges. But he has a sacred duty to perform, and fearlessly will he discharge it. The cause of human freedom and of human rights, and the preservation of our glorious Union, upon which that freedom and those rights depend, require, imperatively require, that this lady, virtuous and benevolent as she may be, shall be torn from her husband and children, and immured with felons in Leverett street Jail, for six months. He intimates, that this is only a portion of the punishment due to the crime of the prisoner. His injured clients are entitled to one thousand dollars from the husband of the lady, and the insulted majesty of the Union claims from the same source satisfaction to the amount of five hundred dollars. After a high-wrought peroration on the obligations of justice and good faith, he calls a witness to prove the guilt of the prisoner. At this point he is interrupted by the opposite counsel, who informs the jury he will not detain them by the examination of witnesses. The prisoner freely, cheerfully admits the act with which she is charged. It is true that she saw in the panting fugitive at her door a representative of HIM who said, "inasmuch as ye did it unto one of the least of these, my brethren, ye did it unto ME." She did take her in, she did feed, and clothe, and lodge, and conceal her. If, in thus obeying the law of God, she had broken that of man, she is willing, if needs be, to suffer bonds in HIS cause who gave His life for her. He then maintains that the Constitution imposes upon the *States* the obligation to surrender fugitives, and gives Congress no authority to visit private individuals with pains and penalties for not assisting in their apprehension. In proof of the correctness of this construction of the Constitution, he reads the opinion of the learned counsel for the prosecution, expressed in his late speech in the Senate. But he rests the defense of the prisoner on higher grounds than constitutional law. He appeals to the LAW OF LOVE written upon the human heart, and proclaimed by the voice of the Son of God, and if the Constitution of the United States abrogates this law, then is it a conspiracy against the virtue of man and the government of Jehovah, and therefore null and void. The cause is submitted by the Court, with a brief intimation to the jury, that in a criminal case they are the judges of the *law* as well as of the fact. The jury, without leaving their box, return a verdict of NOT GUILTY. As the words are caught by the attending multitude, their pent-up feelings find vent in loud and prolonged hurrahs; and the once favorite son of New-England blanches as he hears in the triumphant shouts of the PEOPLE, the knell of his own fame and power.

Be it, that all this is fiction. Alas! it is fiction founded on FACT—founded on Mr. Webster's broken pledges—founded on his open apostasy from the cause of freedom—founded on his proclaimed intention to vote for a law outraging alike the personal security of the citizen and the obligations of the Christian. Mr. Webster treats with disrespect the Legislatures of fourteen States of the free North, which have protested against the extension of slavery to the new territories, not by questioning the binding force of their instructions, but by virtually rebuking them all for expressing "any opinion whatever" in relation to slavery, and by insisting that they "have nothing to do" with a question occupying the thoughts and enlisting the feelings of every citizen, and involving the honor, power and prosperity of our country, and the happiness or degradation of unborn millions of the human race.

He pays a sorry compliment to the common sense of the people in offering to them at the eleventh hour, a new and unheard-of law of "physical geography," together with the "Asiatic scenery and formation" of the conquered territories, as an *excuse* for violating the faith he had plighted, in behalf of the proviso. He has shocked the moral sense of a large portion of the community, by giving in advance his sanction to a law which suspends the liberty or bondage of a citizen on the affidavit of a slaveholder, and the judgment of a postmaster—a law which converts sympathy for guiltless misery into crime, and threatens to tenant our jails with our most estimable men and women.

Mr. Webster underrates the intelligence and moral sensibilities of the masses. Relying on the Southern affinities of our commercial cities, on the subserviency of politicians, on the discipline of party and on his own great influence, Mr. Webster looks *down* upon the people; but the time is probably not far distant when the people will cease to look up to him. Parties will accept of any leaders who can acquire for them the spoils of the day; but in the political history of our country, the people have never placed their affections upon any man, in whose stability and consistency they did not confide.

I remain, dear sir, yours truly,

WILLIAM JAY.

JOHN A. GRAY, PRINTER, 15 SPRUCE STREET.

www.ingramcontent.com/pod-product-compliance
Lightning Source LLC
LaVergne TN
LVHW020640110826
845149LV00004B/1298